Super GOAL

BOOK 1

Manuel dos Santos

Boston   Burr Ridge, IL   Dubuque, IA   Madison, WI   New York   San Francisco   St. Louis
Bangkok   Bogotá   Caracas   Kuala Lumpur   Lisbon   London   Madrid   Mexico City
Milan   Montreal   New Delhi   Santiago   Seoul   Singapore   Sydney   Taipei   Toronto

Editorial Director:	Tina Carver
Senior Managing Editor:	Louis Carrillo
Senior Development Editor:	Janet Battiste
Writing:	Mona Scheraga
Editing:	John Chapman
Art and Design Director:	Heloisa Tiburtius
Book Design:	Heloisa Tiburtius
Cover Design and Production:	Heloisa and Osmarco
Illustrators:	Augusto Freitas, Beatriz Röhrig, Carlos Zubek, Edson Kohatsu, Frank Maciel, Guilherme Rubini, Rogério Coelho, Theo Cordeiro, Tiburcio

McGraw-Hill/Contemporary

A Division of The McGraw·Hill Companies

SuperGoal 1
1st Edition
Workbook

Send all inquiries to:
McGraw-Hill/Contemporary
One Prudential Plaza
130 E. Randolph Street, Suite 400
Chicago, IL 60601

10 09 08 07 06 05 04 03
20 09 08 07 06 05 04 03 02
SF(PMP) BJE

ISBN: 0-07-254334-5

Printed in Singapore

Contents

GOOD MORNING!

A Write the correct expression in each picture.

Good night.
Good evening.

Good morning.
Nice to meet you.

Goodbye.
Hi. How are you?

Fine, thanks. And you?

Laurie, this is Mario!

B Complete the introductions. Use contractions with **be**.

1. This is my friend, Sam. _He's_____ a student.

2. This is my friend, Jane. _____ a student.

3. This is Mr. Lee. _____ an instructor.

4. My name is Paul. _____ a student.

5. This is Ms. White. _____ an instructor.

C Complete the sentences. Use possessive adjectives.

1. He's a student. _His_____ name is Sam.

2. She's a student. _____ name is Jane.

3. He's an instructor. _____ name is Mr. Lee.

4. I'm a student. _____ name is Paul.

5. Welcome, class. I'm Ms. White.

   I'm _____ instructor.

D Complete the introduction.

Paul: Hi. _I'm_____ Paul Wilson.

Jane: Hello, Paul. _____ Jane.

   This is my friend, Sam.

Paul: Nice to meet _____ .

Sam: _____ , too.

   _____ to class.

2

 **WHEN IS YOUR BIRTHDAY?**

A   Write the days of the week in the correct spaces.

May

Sunday

B   Write the months in the right order on the calendar pages below.

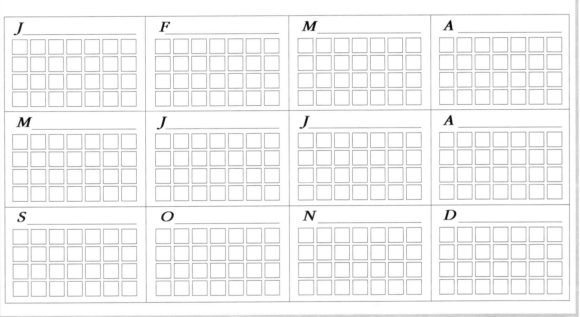

CALENDAR

J_____   F_____   M_____   A_____

M_____   J_____   J_____   A_____

S_____   O_____   N_____   D_____

C   Fill in the numbers.

six, _____seven_____ , eight   two, _____ , four

eight, _____ , ten   ten, _____ , twelve

three, _____ , five   thirteen, _____ , fifteen

D   Match.

1. _____*e*_____ How old are Jim and Jack?   a. We're 8 today.
2. _____ When is their birthday?   b. It's in July.
3. _____ How old are you?   c. They're Jim and Jack.
4. _____ What day is today?   d. It's Monday.
5. _____ What are their names?   e. They're 8.

E   Complete the questions. Use **What, When,** and **How old.**

1. A: _____ are you?   2. A: _____ are their names?
   B: I'm sixteen years old.   B: Susan and Sally.
   A: I'm sixteen, too. We're both sixteen!   A: _____ are they?
   ' _____ is your birthday?   B: They're two months old.
   B: It's in May.
   A: My birthday is in May, too!

F   **WRITING**

Write about yourself.

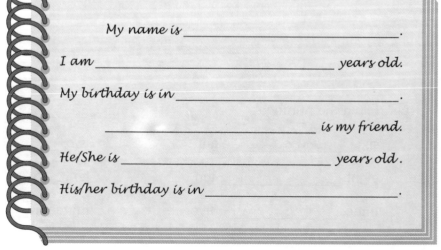

My name is _____.

I am _____ years old.

My birthday is in _____.

_____ is my friend.

He/She is _____ years old.

His/her birthday is in _____.

3 WHAT'S THIS?

A Write the name of each item.

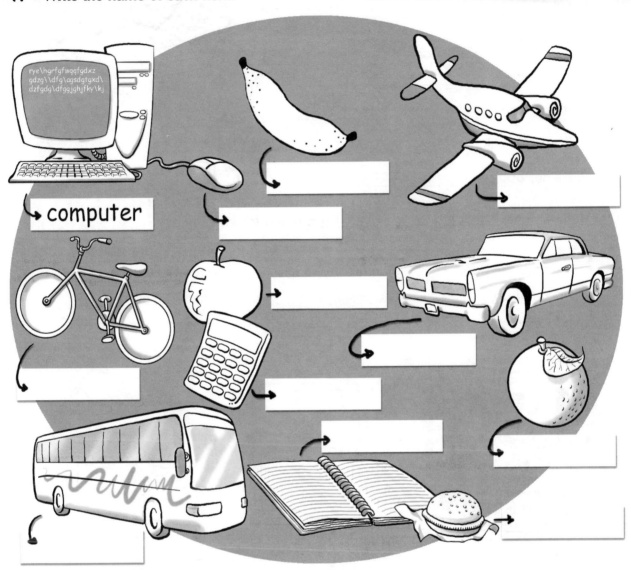

computer

B Write the items from **A** in the correct columns. Use **a** or **an** for each one.

Classroom Items	**Vehicles**	**Food**
1. _a_ _notebook_	1. _a_ _bike_	1. _an_ _orange_
2. ___ _____	2. ___ _____	2. ___ _____
3. ___ _____	3. ___ _____	3. ___ _____
4. ___ _____	4. ___ _____	4. ___ _____

C Change to the plural.

1. What's this? _What are these_ ?

2. It's an apple. _They're apples_ .

3. What's that? _____ ?

4. It's a calculator. _____ .

5. It's a pen. _____ .

6. It's my key. _____ .

7. That's a clock. _____ .

8. It's her book. _____ .

D Write an affirmative (+) or negative (-) command for each picture.

| close the door | give me an orange | open the window |
| ~~stand up~~ | talk | touch the apples |

Please don't stand up.

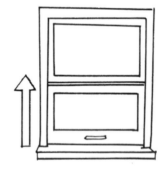

_____

_____

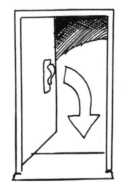

_____

_____

_____

E Complete the conversation. Use ***this***/***these*** for things near the boys.
Use ***that***/***those*** for things not near the boys.

1. *What's this* _____ ?

   It's a watch _____ .

   It's _____ for Dad.

2. *What are those* _____ ?

   They're _____ .

   _____ for Mom.

3. _____ ?

   It's _____ .

   _____ for Mike.

4. _____ ?

   _____ .

   _____ for Fred.

5. _____ ?

   _____ .

   _____ for Sarah.

6. _____ ?

   _____ .

   _____ for you!

F   What's in the museum gift shop? Write your answers here. Use plurals.

1. _____   5. _____
2. _____   6. _____
3. _____   7. _____
4. _____   8. _____

G   Susan is in a museum gift shop. What does she buy? An eraser or a pen for Dad? A clock or a painting for Mom? A CD or a backpack for Carl?

Look at the picture. What are Susan's gifts? Remember **a** or **an.**

1. _____ for Dad   2. _____ for Mom   3. _____ for Carl

H   WRITING

Look at the picture.
Write two lists.

I want	I don't want
_____	_____
_____	_____
_____	_____
_____	_____
_____	_____
_____	_____

WHERE ARE YOU FROM?

A Read about the people at the parade. Write the answers to Bob's questions.

Maria and Paolo are from Rome, Italy. They're at a parade in New York City. Kim is from Korea, and Nigel and Milton are from London. Alberto is from Argentina. Bob, the reporter, is from New York.

Bob: Hello. Are you from the United States?

Alberto: No, _____ . I'm from _____ .

Bob: Welcome! Are you from Argentina?

Maria and Paolo: _____ , _____ . We're _____ .

Bob: Are you from Florence, Italy?

Maria and Paolo: No, _____ . _____ Rome.

Bob: And where are you from? Are you from Japan?

Kim: _____ , _____ . I'm _____ .

Bob: Are you two from Canada?

Nigel and Milton: No, _____ . _____ TV reporters
in _____ .

Bob: Well, welcome to New York! It's a small world!

B Write the questions.

1. _Where is she from_ ?
   Alexandra is from Egypt.

2. _____ ?
   She's seventeen years old.

3. _____ ?
   It's 14 Park Street.

4. _____ ?
   It's (555) 121-4343.

5. _____ ?
   She's in Washington now.

C Complete the questions. Then answer the questions. Use the information in **B**.

1. _Is_ _____ Alexandra from the United States?
   No, she isn't. She's from Egypt.

2. _____ Alexandra sixteen years old?
   _____

3. _____ her address 14 Park Street?
   _____

4. _____ her telephone number (555) 122-4343?
   _____

5. _____ she in Egypt now?
   _____

D These sentences are not true. Make these sentences negative.

1. Alexandra is in Egypt.   _Alexandra isn't in Egypt._

2. Alexandra is American.   _____

3. Alexandra is from Los Angeles. _____

4. Alexandra is fourteen years old. _____

5. Her address is 40 Park Street.   _____

E Fill in the correct form of **be**. Circle the correct preposition.

Paula: Hi. My name _____is_____ Paula. What's your name?

Mike: I' _____ Mike. This _____ my girlfriend, Marnie.

She' _____ **in/from** Australia, but she lives in the United States now.

Marnie: Hi. _____ you from San Francisco, Paula?

Paula: No, _____ not. I'm **from/in** Austin.

Marnie: _____ Austin in California?

Paula: No, it _____ . It's in Texas. Are you **from/in** San Francisco?

Mike: No, I' _____ . We're **in/from** San Francisco for the race today.

We live in Los Angeles.

F Answer the questions. Use short answers.
For negative answers, write the correct information.

1. Is Paula Mike's girlfriend?

   No, she isn't. Marnie is Mike's girlfriend.

2. Is Paula from Austin?

   _____

3. Is Marnie from Austin?

   _____

4. Is Austin in California?

   _____

5. Are they in Texas now?

   _____

G WRITING

Complete the form. Write about yourself.

SCHOOL INFORMATION FORM

Name: _____   _____
              First Name   *Last Name*

Address: _____   _____
                Number   *Street*

_____   _____   _____
        City   *State*   *Zip Code*

Telephone: _____

E-mail: _____

Age: _____

H WRITING

Write about two friends.
Answer these questions.

1. What is your friend's name?

2. Where is your friend from?

3. What is the name of your
   friend's city or town?

4. Is your friend on e-mail?
   What is his/her e-mail address?

Friend 1
_____
_____
_____
_____
_____
_____
_____

Friend 2
_____
_____
_____
_____
_____
_____

REVIEW for Units 1 to 4

A Complete the questions. Choose from **What, When, Where, How old.**
Then match each question with its correct answer.

_g_	1. _Where_ are you from?		a. My school is in Florida.
___	2. _____ is your birthday?		b. He's twenty years old.
___	3. _____ day is today?		c. My house is on Park Avenue.
___	4. _____ are you?		d. My birthday is in December.
___	5. _____ is your house?		e. It's September.
___	6. _____ month is this?		f. Today is Monday.
___	7. _____ is your school?		g. I'm from the United States.
___	8. _____ is your brother?		h. I'm seventeen.

B Write the negative.

1. Sit down.   _Don't sit down._ _____

2. Please close the door. _____

3. Today is Sunday.   _____

4. He is from Brazil.   _____

5. They are sisters.   _____

6. I am ten years old.   _____

C Change the statements to questions. Use real information.

1. Today is (day of week).   _Is today Tuesday?_ _____

2. It's (month and day) today. _____

3. (name) is 17 years old.   _____

4. You're from (country).   _____

5. You're (nationality).   _____

6. That's your book.   _____

7. Those are our desks.   _____

8. That's a famous painting.   _____

D Complete the crossword puzzle. Use the clues on the right.

1				2		3

ACROSS

1. greeting
4. he, she, _____
6. weekend day
9. Sit _____ .

DOWN

1. she/her, he/_____
2. month
3. day of the week
5. _____ is your name?
7. You _____ I are friends.
8. We _____ students.
10. How _____ are you?
11. opposite of **yes**

E Write the correct form of the verb **be**.

Today _____ Monday. It _____ the first day of school. Mr. Alvarez

and his students _____ in class. There _____ twenty students and

twenty-one desks. One desk _____ for Mr. Alvarez.

"How old _____ you, Brandon?" asks Mr. Alvarez. Brandon

_____ sixteen years old. The students _____ all 16 or 17 years old.

Mr. Alvarez _____ seventeen years old. He _____ thirty-five.

It_____ his birthday today. "I _____ thirty-five years old today,"

says Mr. Alvarez. The students say, "Happy Birthday, Mr. Alvarez!"

GOOD MORNING!

Think about what you know. Check (✓) the column.

	I can do this. (+)	I need to study this more. (?)
Say hello.		
Say goodbye.		
Ask and answer: *How are you?*		
Say my name.		
Make an introduction.		
Use the verb *be—I am, you are, he is, she is.*		
Use possessive adjectives: *my, your, his, her.*		

What do you know now? _____

_____

_____

WHEN IS YOUR BIRTHDAY?

Think about what you know. Check (✓) the column.

	I can do this. (+)	I need to study this more. (?)
Say the names of the days of the week.		
Say the names of the months of the year.		
Count from 1 to 20.		
Ask and answer: *What day is today? What month is it?*		
Ask and answer: *How old are you?*		
Ask and answer: *When is your birthday?*		
Use the verb *be—we are, you are, they are.*		
Use the possessive adjectives: *our, your, their.*		
Use the question words: *What, When, How old.*		

What do you know now? _____

_____

_____

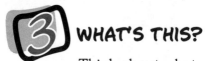

3 WHAT'S THIS?

Think about what you know. Check (✓) the column.

	I can do this. (+)	I need to study this more. (?)
Say the names of things in the classroom.		
Ask and answer: *What's this/that?*		
Give commands and instructions.		
Use articles: *a/an, the.*		
Use the pronouns: *this/that, these/those.*		
Use plural nouns.		
Use imperatives.		

What do you know now? _____

_____

_____

4 WHERE ARE YOU FROM?

Think about what you know. Check (✓) the column.

	I can do this. (+)	I need to study this more. (?)
Say the names of countries and nationalities.		
Say the numbers from 1 to 100.		
Ask and answer: *Where are you from? Are you (English)?*		
Give your address, telephone number, and e-mail address.		
Make negative sentences with the verb *be* (*I'm not French*).		
Ask and answer *yes/no* questions with the verb *be* (*Is he French? No, he isn't.*).		

What do you know now? _____

_____

_____

WHO'S IN YOUR FAMILY?

A Answer *yes* or *no*.

1. _____ Susan is Sam's wife.

2. _____ Eric is Tina's son.

3. _____ Rose is Eric's sister.

4. _____ Ed is Sara's grandfather.

B Complete the sentences. Who is Sam?

1. He's Jennifer's _____ .

2. He's Tina's _____ .

3. He's Susan's _____ .

4. He's Eric's _____ .

C Who are you in your family? Look at **A** and **B** for ideas. Who am I?

Example: I'm Julia's son.

1. I'm _____ .

2. I'm _____ .

3. I'm _____ .

4. I'm _____ .

5. I'm _____ .

D Write the possessive.

1. The son of Ed   *Ed's son*

2. The aunt of Susan   _____

3. The father of the girl   _____

4. The father of the children   _____

5. The mother of the boys   _____

6. The dogs of the aunts   _____

E Complete the sentences.
Use **have, has, don't have,** or **doesn't have.**
Use the information in **A.**

1. Sam *has* _____ two sisters.

2. Eric and Jennifer _____ three children.

3. Sam _____ brothers.

4. Sara _____ one sister.

5. Ed and Tina _____ three children.

F Here are the answers. What are the questions?

1. *How many brothers does Sam have?*
_____
Sam doesn't have brothers.

2. _____?
Sam has two sisters.

3. _____?
Tina has four grandchildren.

4. _____?
Rose and Bill have one child.

G Here are the answers. What are the questions?

1. *Who's Sam's aunt?*
_____
Sam's aunt is Rose.

2. _____?
Sam's mother is Jennifer.

3. _____?
Sam's father is Eric.

4. _____?
Sam's grandparents are Ed and Tina.

H READING

Clerk: What's your name?

Child: Delores.

Clerk: What's your last name?

Child: Ruiz.

Clerk: What's your father's name?

Child: Daddy.

Clerk: O.K. What's your address?

Child: Main Street.

Clerk: What's your telephone number?

Child: I don't know.

Mother: There you are, Delores! Thank you, Ms. . . . ?

Clerk: Ms. Jones. Please teach Delores her address and telephone number.

Mother: Yes, Ms. Jones. Thank you.

Write *yes* or *no*.

1. _____ Delores is the clerk's daughter.

2. _____ Delores is Mrs. Ruiz's daughter.

3. _____ Delores knows her address.

4. _____ Delores knows her telephone number.

5. _____ Delores says her father's name.

I WRITING

Write about your family. Answer these questions.

1. How many brothers and sisters do you have?

2. What are their names?

3. How old are your brothers and sisters?

4. Who is the baby in your family?

5. What are your grandparents' names?

6. How many aunts do you have?

7. How many uncles do you have?

8. Your aunts' children are your cousins. How many cousins do you have?

9. Do you have a pet?

10. What is your pet's name?

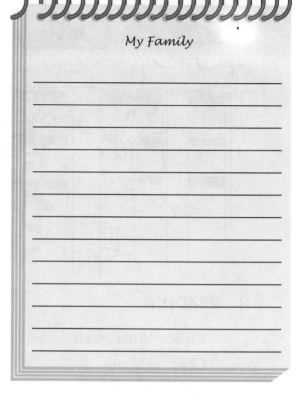

My Family

J   Complete the sentences.
Then write the words in the puzzle.

1. My mother's mother is my

_____ .

2. My parents' child is their daughter or

_____ .

3. My uncle's wife is my

_____ .

4. My father is my mother's

_____ .

5. My mother's brother is my

_____ .

6. My mother and father are my

_____ .

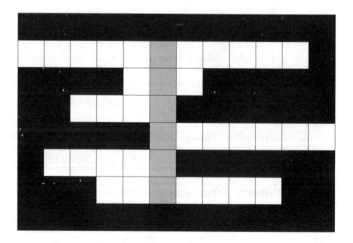

What is the mystery word?
Look at the dark boxes.
Read down.

_____

 **IS THERE A GARDEN?**

A Write the names of the items in the blanks.

1. _____

2. _____

3. _____

4. _____

5. _____

6. _____

7. _____

8. _____

9. _____

10. _____

B Complete the sentences.
Use **behind, in front of, under, on,** or **in.**

1. The mirror is _____ the bathroom.

2. The backpack is _____ the closet.

3. The rug is _____ the table.

4. The flowers are _____ the table.

5. The big chair is _____ the TV.

6. The dog is _____ the kitchen.

7. The dog is _____ the refrigerator.

8. The lamp is _____ the table.

9. The books are _____ the bed.

10. The cat is _____ the bed.

C Complete the conversation. John is a movie actor.
Use *there is, there are, is there,* and *are there.*

Reporter: Is your house in Hollywood big?

John: Yes, _____ _____ 35 rooms.

Reporter: Thirty-five rooms? That is a big house!

John: Yes, _____ _____ 10 bedrooms,

and _____ _____ 12 bathrooms.

_____ _____ a kitchen upstairs, and _____

_____ a kitchen downstairs.

Reporter: _____ _____ a pool?

John: Yes, _____ _____ two pools. _____

_____ one pool in the house,

and _____ _____ one pool behind the house.

Reporter: _____ _____ famous paintings?

John: Yes, I have two paintings by Picasso.

Reporter: That's great. _____ _____ a garden?

John: Yes, _____ _____ a large garden with flowers

behind the house.

Reporter: What's your favorite room?

John: It's my bedroom. _____ _____ two phones,

a computer, and a big-screen TV in my bedroom. I watch myself on TV!

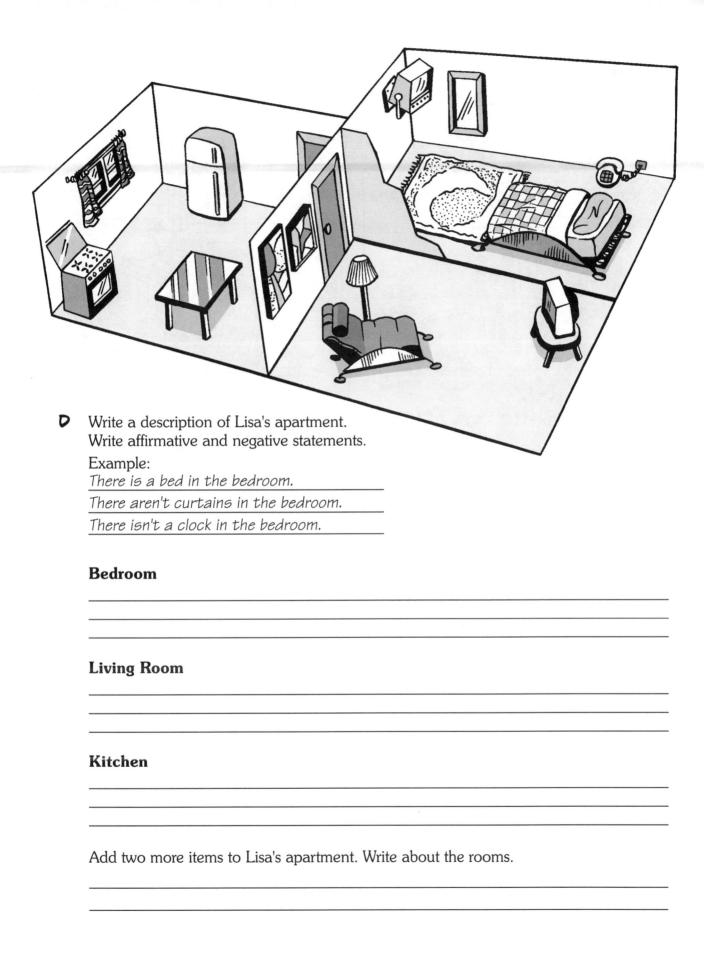

D Write a description of Lisa's apartment.
Write affirmative and negative statements.

Example:

There is a bed in the bedroom.

There aren't curtains in the bedroom.

There isn't a clock in the bedroom.

Bedroom

_____

_____

_____

Living Room

_____

_____

_____

Kitchen

_____

_____

_____

Add two more items to Lisa's apartment. Write about the rooms.

_____

_____

E READING

Friendship Hotel

*Welcome to Friendship Hotel. It's a great place. The rooms are big and comfortable.
All the rooms have a TV, two beds, a desk, two chairs, and a table.
The bathroom is very big, and there is also a large closet. There are telephones
in all the bathrooms. Many rooms have a window with a view of the ocean.
Downstairs there is a gift shop, and upstairs there is a rooftop garden.
Behind the hotel, there is a swimming pool for hotel guests.*

Answer *yes* or *no*.

1. _____ The rooms in the hotel are small.

2. _____ All the rooms have one bed, one chair, and a desk.

3. _____ The bathroom is big, but there isn't a closet.

4. _____ There is a pool in front of the hotel.

5. _____ Many rooms have windows with a view of the museum.

F WRITING

Write about your dream bedroom.
Answer the questions.

1. Is there a big bed or a small bed?

2. What other furniture is there?

3. Are there windows?

4. Is there a view?

5. Are there special things in the room?

My Dream Bedroom

My dream bedroom is just right for me.

_____

_____

_____

_____

_____

_____

WHERE'S THE MALL?

A   What are these words? They're places! Write the words in the puzzle.

1. laml

2. toshpial

3. karp

4. ketpusrmare

5. loshoc

6. tausertnar

7. tolhe

A
I
R
P
O
R
T

B   Make a conversation.
Write the sentences in the correct order.

Excuse me. Is there a restaurant near here?

Go to the corner, and turn right.

Thank you.

Yes, there's one across from the post office.

And where is the post office?

You're welcome.

A: _Excuse me._ _____

B: _____

A: _____

B: _____

A: _____

B: _____

BUS STATION		MOVIE THEATER	MALL		DRUGSTORE

MAIN AVENUE

BROADWAY

HOSPITAL		HOTEL		FRANKLIN STREET	SUPERMARKET
	BANK	RESTAURANT			

PARK AVENUE

SCHOOL	PARK		BOOKSTORE

C Complete the sentences. Use *across from, between,* and *next to.*

1. The hotel is _____ the bank and the restaurant.

2. The mall is _____ the restaurant.

3. The movie theater is _____ the mall.

D Answer the questions. Make two sentences for each.

1. Where's the restaurant? _____ .

_____ .

2. Where's the bank? _____ .

_____ .

3. Where's the supermarket? _____ .

_____ .

E Look at the picture. Complete the conversation. Help the tourist. She's at the bookstore.

Tourist: Excuse me. Where is the hospital?

You: _____ straight head to the next corner.

_____ right at the school.

The hospital is _____ the school. It's _____ the school and the bus station.

Tourist: Thank you.

26

F READING

BEAUTIFUL PENANG

Penang is a small island off the coast of Malaysia in Southeast Asia. About a million people live on this lovely island, and thousands of tourists visit every year. There's a lot to see and do in Penang. There are miles of sunny beaches with smooth white sand. Tourists stay in small friendly hotels on the beach or in big hotels in the town. There are old temples and many beautiful parks. There are also many places to shop. And Penang even has its own shopping mall on Penang Road. It's called KOMTAR and has over 200 stores.

Answer *yes* or *no*. For no answers, write a correct sentence.

1. *No* _____ Penang is in South America.

   Penang is in Malaysia. _____

2. _____ Many tourists visit Penang every year.

   _____

3. _____ There aren't many stores in Penang.

   _____

4. _____ There are no big hotels in Penang.

   _____

5. _____ KOMTAR is the name of a famous hotel.

   _____

6. _____ There are hotels on the beaches.

   _____

7. _____ There are no parks in Penang.

   _____

G Is there a mall near your house? Are there good streets for shopping near you? Draw a map. Write the names of the stores on the map.

H WRITING

Write about your city.

1. Is the city old or modern?

2. Is the city big or small?

3. Is it popular with tourists?

4. Are there many tourist attractions?

5. What are the attractions?

6. Are there famous restaurants?

7. Are there many stores?

8. What is the name of the most popular shopping street or mall?

9. Are there beaches in your city?

10. Is there an airport near the city?

My City

8 WHAT ARE YOU DOING?

A Complete the conversation. Use the present progressive forms with contractions. Use the verbs in the box.

drink	eat	have	cook	talk

The Adams family and the Morgan family are having a barbecue in the Morgans' backyard. Mr. Morgan's daughter, Pam, is calling from college. She's speaking to her brother George.

Pam: Hi. It's Pam. What's happening?

George: _We're having_ a barbecue.

Pam: Great! What's Dad doing?

George: _____ hot dogs.

Pam: And Mom?

George: _____ to Mrs. Adams.

Pam: Are the Adams' daughters there?

George: Yes. _____ hamburgers.

Pam: And what about you?

George: Well, Pam, _____ a soda,

and I'm _____ to you!

B   Complete the questions and answers.

1. *What is he eating*   ?

    He's eating a sandwich   .

4. What _____ reading?

_____ a book.

2. What _____ listening to?

_____ the stereo.

5. What _____ ?

_____ basketball on TV.

3. Where _____ ?

_____ under a tree.

6. What _____ ?

_____ in the park.

C Where are they? Circle the phrase with the correct preposition.

1. (in the yard)
   at the yard

2. in the corner
   on the corner

3. in their bikes
   on their bikes

4. in the movie theater
   near the movie theater

5. in the movie theater
   near the movie theater

6. at the bus stop
   on the bus stop

D Look at the pictures in **C.** Describe the actions.

1. *They're sitting in the yard.* _____

2. _____

3. _____

4. _____

5. _____

6. _____

E Change these sentences to the plural.

1. The child is playing in the park.   *The children are playing in the park.*

2. The woman is eating in a restaurant.   _____

3. The man is sitting in the café.   _____

4. The girl is waiting on the corner.   _____

A Day at the Beach

F What are they doing? Describe the scene. Complete these sentences.

1. The woman in the restaurant _____ .

2. The man next to her _____ .

3. The boy on the beach _____ .

4. The woman on the beach _____ .

5. The man next to her _____ .

G WRITING

Imagine you are in the picture. Write to a friend. Complete the sentences.

Dear_____ ,

I'm sitting in a restaurant at the beach.

I'm _____ . A man near me _____ .

_____ . _____

_____ . _____ .

I'm having a lot of fun.

Love,

_____

A Read. Then answer the questions about the family.

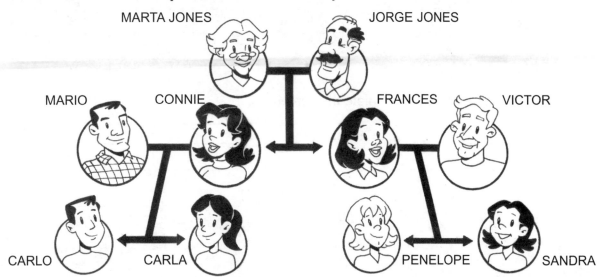

Carlo and Carla are brother and sister. Their father, Mario, has two brothers. He has no sisters. Their mother, Connie, has no brothers, but she has a sister, Frances. Frances's husband's name is Victor. Frances and Victor have two children, Penelope and Sandra. The two families live in a big house with Connie and Frances's parents, Marta and Jorge.

1. How many children do Mario and Connie have?
   _They have two children._____.

2. What are their children's names?
   _____.

3. How many aunts do Carlo and Carla have?
   _____.

4. Does Mario have a brother?
   _____.

5. Penelope and Sandra have an uncle. What's his name?
   _____.

6. Who are Carlo and Carla's grandparents?
   _____.

B Rewrite these sentences with plural nouns. Make other necessary changes.

1. That man is my uncle.   _Those men are my uncles._____
2. Where is the newspaper?   _____
3. Is there a child in the room?   _____
4. Is that person your friend?   _____
5. Who is that woman?   _____

C What are they doing? Complete the sentences.

1. _____ in a restaurant. 3. _____ on the telephone.

2. _____ to the radio. 4. _____ a letter.

D Fill in the blanks. Use *next to, on, across from, between,* and *in front of.*

1. The three people are _____ the movie theater.

2. The "Disco Tonight" sign is _____ the movie theater.

3. The ice cream parlor is _____ the movie theater.

4. The ice cream parlor is _____ the movie theater and the jeans store.

5. The video store is _____ the movie theater.

E One boy is using his cell phone. Complete the conversation.
Choose from *next to, on, across from, near, turn left,* and *there's.*

Boy: Walk down Park Avenue. _____ at Main Street. The movie theater is
_____ the video store on Main Street.

Friend: I'm hungry. Is there a restaurant _____ the store?

Boy: Yes. _____ an ice cream parlor _____ the movie theater.

Friend: Is there a good movie tonight?

Boy: There's a sign _____ the movie theater that says "Disco Tonight."

Friend: Sounds great! See you soon.

34

WHO'S IN YOUR FAMILY?

Think about what you know. Check (✓) the column.

	I can do this. (+)	I need to study this more. (?)
Say the words for relatives.		
Talk about the people in your family.		
Ask and answer: *How many brothers/sisters do you have?*		
Use the verb have *(I have two brothers. Do you have a sister?)*.		
Use the possessive 's *(my sister's dog)*.		
Use the question words: *How many, Who.*		

What do you know now? _____

_____

_____

IS THERE A GARDEN?

Think about what you know. Check (✓) the column.

	I can do this. (+)	I need to study this more. (?)
Say the words for rooms in the house.		
Say the words for items in the house.		
Talk about your home.		
Ask and answer: *Is there a (sofa in the living room)?*		
Tell about locations: *There is a cat under the table.*		
Use *there is/there are (Is there a TV in the kitchen? No, there isn't.).*		
Prepositions of place: *behind, in, in front of, on, under.*		

What do you know now? _____

_____

_____

35

WHERE'S THE MALL?

Think about what you know. Check (✓) the column.

	I can do this. (+)	I need to study this more. (?)
Say the names of places in a city/town.		
Ask for directions to a place.		
Give directions to a place.		
Use imperatives for directions *(turn left/right, go straight)*.		
Use the prepositions of place: *across from, between, far from, next to, near, on.*		

What do you know now? _____

_____

_____

WHAT ARE YOU DOING?

Think about what you know. Check (✓) the column.

	I can do this. (+)	I need to study this more. (?)
Use common action verbs (examples: *watch, talk, read*).		
Talk about what you're doing.		
Ask and answer: *What are you doing?*		
Use the present progressive tense.		
Use the prepositions of place: *at, in, on.*		
Use irregular plurals *(man—men, woman—women, person—people).*		

What do you know now? _____

_____

_____

 **WHAT DO YOU DO?**

A What words complete the sentences? Write the words in the crossword puzzle.

ACROSS

5. Deborah takes pictures. She's a _____ .

7. Tom sells things. He's a _____ .

8. My father sings. He's a _____ .

9. Tina and Tim are actors. They _____ in movies.

DOWN

1. Jim writes for a newspaper. He's a _____ .

2. Rita and Jane work in a hospital. They're _____ .

3. Kim and Lee are dog walkers. They _____ dogs.

4. Mohammed drives a taxi. He's a taxi _____ .

5. Louis and Janet work for the airlines. They're _____ .

6. My sister is on TV. She's an _____ .

LAURIE

GINA AND RALPH

JOE AND ELAINE

MIKE, CAROL,
AND MARIA

B   Complete the questions and answers.

1. A: (Joe) *What does Joe do?*
   B: He _walks_ _____ dogs.

2. A: (Elaine) _____
   B: She _____ pictures.

3. A: (Laurie) _____
   B: She _____ clothing.

4. A: (Gina) _____
   B: She _____ food.

5. A: (Ralph) _____
   B: He's a _____

6. A: (Gina and Ralph) _____
   B: They _____ in a restaurant.

7. A: (Carol and Maria) _____
   B: They _____ taxis.

8. A: (Mike) _____
   B: He _____ magazines.

38

C Complete the conversation. Use the information in the picture.

Paula: Hi. I'm Paula Carter. I'm a _____ . I work for a newspaper.

Marty: That's sounds like a great job. I'm Marty Collins.

Paula: What _____ you _____ ?

Marty: I'm a _____ . And my wife's a _____ .
She's not here. She's at work.

Paula: Do you know anyone here?

Marty: Yes, I do. Those are my friends, Kevin and Bill.

Paula: What _____ they _____ ?

Marty: _____ hairdressers. _____ at "Cuts for Kids."
Kevin's wife _____ a chef.
She _____ at the Italian restaurant
on Main Street. She isn't here. She's at work, too.

What do you do? Write about yourself. Use the space in the picture.

D Circle the correct answers.

A: What (do/does) Linda do?

B: She ('re/'s) a teacher.

A: What do your parents (do/are) ?

B: They (do/'re) teachers.

A: What does Roger (do/does)?

B: He (fly/flies) a plane.

A: What (does/is) your sister do?

B: She (does/'s) a student.

E READING

Angela's Restaurant

Angela has a new restaurant, and she's the chef. She works six days a week. Angela has some helpers at the restaurant. Alex also works at the restaurant. He's a waiter and a part-time student. He works three days a week. Leonard is also a waiter. He works six nights a week. He's a salesperson at a clothing store in the afternoon.

Today a photographer is taking pictures of the new restaurant. Her name is Ellen, and she works for a newspaper. Jerry is writing about the restaurant for the newspaper. Angela is really happy. She wants many new customers.

Answer *yes* or *no*.

1. _____ Angela works for a newspaper.

2. _____ Ellen is a photographer.

3. _____ Alex works three days a week.

4. _____ Leonard is a waiter.

5. _____ Jerry is an actor.

F WRITING

Write about your family members and their jobs.

1. What do they do?

2. Where do they work?

3. Do they have part-time jobs?

4. How many hours a week do they work?

5. What days do they work?

6. Do they work at night?

7. What do they do on Saturdays and Sundays?

Family Members' Jobs

WHAT DOES HE LOOK LIKE?

A Lee is a new student. He is talking to Gail. Complete the conversation.
Use the verbs **play, teach, ride**, and **work.** Use short answers.

Lee: Who's that?

Gail: That's Peter. He _____ in a rock group.

Lee: _____ he _____ the guitar?

Gail: No, he _____ . He _____ the drums. He's very good.

He even _____ music lessons at the community center.

Lee: Do your friends have jobs after school?

Gail: Yes, they _____ . Maria _____ in a café,

and Gary _____ at a store.

Lee: Who is that tall boy over there?

Gail: That's Arnold. We _____ the same bus to school.

Lee: _____ he _____ in the band too?

Gail: Yes, he _____ . He _____ the guitar.

And that's Jerome. He doesn't _____ in the band.

He just _____ basketball!

B Make a conversation between Gail and Lee. Number the sentences in the correct order.

_____1_____ Lee: Who's that?

_____ Lee: Does she play any sports?

_____ Lee: Does he play on the school team?

_____ Lee: What does she do?

_____ Gail: Yes, he does. And his sister is my best friend.

_____ Gail: She sells clothing in a store.

_____ Gail: That's Andrew. He plays soccer.

_____ Gail: No, she doesn't. She works after school every day.

C Write the words in the correct order to make sentences.

1. doesn't speak he English

   _He doesn't speak English_____ .

2. study you do French

   _____ ?

3. Ms. Lee science teach does

   _____ ?

4. don't Spanish take we

   _____ .

5. long hair has blond she

   _____ .

6. carries red a Ted backpack

   _____ .

7. black has Mary hair long

   _____ .

8. CD player new has Ricki a

   _____ .

LARRY   MISSY   PEDRO   AMY   JUAN

D One of the people in the picture is Carla's friend.

  1. Carla's friend doesn't wear glasses. Her friend has long blond hair.
     What's the name of her friend?

    _____

  2. One of the people in the picture is Peter's friend. His friend has short black hair and
     wears glasses. His friend doesn't ride a bicycle. What's the name of his friend?

    _____

E Imagine the people in the picture are your friends. Describe them to someone else.

  1. Juan _____

    _____

  2. Amy _____

    _____

  3. Pedro _____

    _____

  4. Missy _____

    _____

  5. Larry _____

    _____

F   Read the text. Write the name next to each person in the teacher's room.

Ms. Fletcher is the history teacher. She has blond hair and blue eyes. She also wears glasses. Mrs. Collins teaches French. She's short, and she has black hair. The math teacher is Mr. Argano. He's very intelligent. He doesn't have any hair. Mr. Johnson is tall and has black hair. He's the gym teacher. Mr. Werner teaches science. He has white hair, and he isn't very tall. He's very nice. Mrs. Maple is tall. She teaches cooking classes.

G WRITING

Write an e-mail to a friend. Write about your school.

1. What subjects do you take?

2. What is your favorite class?

3. Who are your teachers?

4. Do they give a lot of homework?

5. Do you do your homework with your friends?

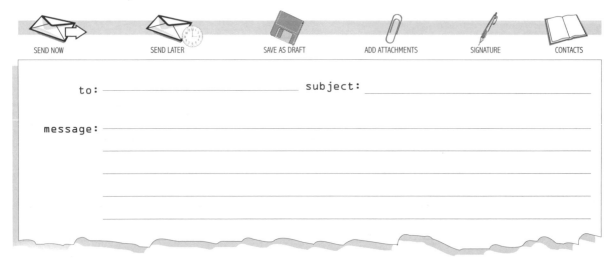

WHAT TIME DO YOU GET UP?

A Look at the pictures, and complete the sentences.
Use the present tense or the present progressive.

1. Mr. Carter usually gets up at 6:00, but today _____ .

_____ .

4. Mr. Carter usually drives, but tonight

_____ .

2. He usually _____ in the kitchen, but today he's having breakfast in the dining room.

5. The Carters usually _____ _____ at home, but today they're eating in a restaurant.

3. Mr. Carter's children usually _____ _____ at school, but today they're doing it at home.

6. Mr. Carter usually _____ _____ at 11:00, but tonight he's going to bed early.

45

B   Fill in the correct word. Use *at, before, after, then, in,* and *on.*

My sister always has breakfast _____ 7:00 A.M. _____ breakfast, she goes to the gym.

She goes to work _____ 9:00. She drinks a lot of coffee _____ the morning at work. She does a lot of work _____ lunch.

She eats lunch _____ noon. _____ lunch, she sometimes takes a walk. She sometimes eats an apple _____ the afternoon.

_____ work, she goes home. She takes a shower and has a soda. _____ she makes dinner.

She usually watches TV_____ the evening.

She always goes to the movies _____ Friday night.

C   Unscramble these sentences.

1. eats she noon at always

   _____.

2. in the afternoon teeth brushes he his never

   _____.

3. eats sometimes he 6:00 at

   _____.

4. usually do I homework home at my

   _____.

5. exercise always we breakfast before

   _____.

D   How often to you do these things? Use *always, usually, sometimes,* and *never.*

1. get up before 6 A.M.   4. write e-mail to my family members

   _____   _____

2. do homework with friends   5. study for tests at night

   _____   _____

3. brush my teeth after breakfast

   _____

E Jaime has three part-time jobs. He also plays tennis. Read Jaime's weekday schedule. Then complete the sentences below.

Use these adverbs of frequency: **always, usually, sometimes, never.**
Use these time expressions: **before, after, every day, at, in, on.**

Jaime's Schedule

	MONDAY	TUESDAY	WEDNESDAY	THURSDAY	FRIDAY
6:00-10:00 A.M.	Drive taxi	Drive taxi	Drive taxi	Drive taxi	Drive taxi
10:00 A.M - 11:30 A.M.	Teach Spanish	Teach Spanish	10:00 A.M.- 2:00 P.M. Work at Startime Coffee Café	Teach Spanish	Teach Spanish
Noon -1:00 P.M.	Play tennis with Kathy	Play tennis with Kathy	Play tennis with Kathy	Play tennis with George	
2:00 - 6:00 P.M.	Free time	Free time	Free time	Free time	Free time
7:00 -11:00 P.M.	Work at Startime Coffee Café		Work at Startime Coffee Café	Work at Startime Coffee Café	Work at Startime Coffee Café
12:00 P.M.- 1:00 A.M.	Watch TV	Watch TV	Watch TV	Watch TV	Watch TV

1. Jaime _always_ drives the taxi _in_ the morning.

2. He _____ drives the taxi _____ his Spanish lessons.

3. He _____ plays tennis _____ his Spanish lessons.

4. He drives the taxi _____ .

5. He _____ teaches Spanish _____ Wednesday.

6. Jaime _____ plays tennis _____ night.

47

F Read the article about Angela.

Angela's Day

It's 5 A.M. Is Angela at home sleeping? No, she is at the market. She's buying food for her restaurant. Angela goes to the market six days a week. Then, at 6:30, she goes to the gym and exercises. At 7:30, she goes home and goes back to bed.

Angela goes back to the restaurant at 1 P.M. She cooks the food for the day. She writes out the menu for the next day. The restaurant is open from 5 P.M. to 11 P.M. After 11, Angela cleans up the restaurant and the kitchen. She goes home at midnight. And the next morning she gets up at 5 again.

But on Sundays she doesn't get up before 8 A.M. The restaurant isn't open on Sundays. Does Angela cook on Sundays? No, she doesn't. She goes out to eat in a restaurant of course!

Answer *yes* or *no*.

1. _____ Angela goes to the market at 6:30 A.M.

2. _____ Angela sleeps in the morning after gym.

3. _____ Angela goes to her restaurant at 2 P.M.

4. _____ Angela goes home at 11 P.M.

5. _____ Angela eats in her restaurant on Sundays.

G WRITING

Write about your days.
Use time expressions and adverbs of frequency.

1. What do you do before school?

2. What do you usually do after school?

3. When do you do your homework?

4. What days do you see your friends?

5. When do you watch TV?

My Days

48

 **CAN YOU SWIM?**

A Complete the sentences.

1. Gloria likes to _____.

2. Mike and Ken like to _____.

3. Paul likes to _____.

4. Ben and Andy like to _____.

5. Alice likes to _____.

6. Julio and Paco like to _____.

B Which of the following activities **do you like/don't you like?**

| to dance | to sing | to do homework | to eat | to play basketball | to ride a bike |
| to swim | to cook | to ride a horse | to run | to read | to talk on the phone |

I like to swim. _____

_____

_____

_____

Your ideas:

_____

I don't like to talk on the phone. _____

_____

_____

_____

_____

C Write sentences about John and Debbie. Use **can** or **can't.** Use the following verbs: **play basketball, play chess, ride a bicycle, skateboard.**

John

1. _____
2. _____
3. _____

Debbie

1. _____
2. _____
3. _____

John and Debbie _____

D Complete the sentences. Use **likes to, like to, doesn't like to,** or **don't like to.**

1. John _____ ride horses.
2. Debbie _____ ride horses
3. John _____ fish.
4. Debbie _____ fish.
5. Debbie and John _____ jog.
6. They _____ swim.

E Alice is talking about her boyfriend. Look at the pictures and complete the story.
Use the words in the box.

beach	favorite	to study	to dance	boyfriend	like	to swim	stores

Johnny is my _____ . He and I _____ to do the same things. We both
like to go to parties, and we love _____ . We like to go to the _____ ,
too. We both like _____ . The shopping mall is a _____ place for us,
too. We love to look in the _____ and eat junk food. But there is one problem.
Johnny likes _____ and I don't.

F Which of the following activities can you do? Which can't you do?

to dance	to sing	to surf	to ride a bike
to swim	to cook	to ride a horse	to play the piano

I can sing. _____   *I can't cook.* _____

_____   _____

_____   _____

_____   _____

Your ideas:

_____   _____

G READING

The Cousins

Julio lives in San Juan, Puerto Rico. He likes to sing and dance and listen to CDs, but he doesn't like sports. His friends like to go to the mall, but he doesn't. He likes to watch TV, but he really doesn't like movies. He doesn't often go to museums, but he likes to look at modern sculpture.

Julio's cousin Jose lives in Philadelphia, Pennsylvania. He likes sports. He plays tennis every day. He goes to baseball games and watches soccer games on TV. He never sings or dances, but he does listen to CDs. He likes to go to the movies and to watch TV, but he doesn't like shopping malls. He often goes to museums, and he likes to look at modern painting.

1. Does Jose like sports?

_____

2. Does Julio like to sing and dance?

_____

3. Do the cousins like shopping malls?

_____

4. What do you think that the cousins do when Julio goes to Philadelphia?

_____

5. How are the cousins the same? How are they different?

_____

H WRITING

Tell what you like and don't like to do.

1. What is your favorite activity?

2. Where do you do it?

3. When do you do it?

4. Who do you do it with?

5. What don't you like to do?

6. Why don't you like this activity?

What I Like and Don't Like

A Look at the pictures. Answer the questions. Write complete sentences.

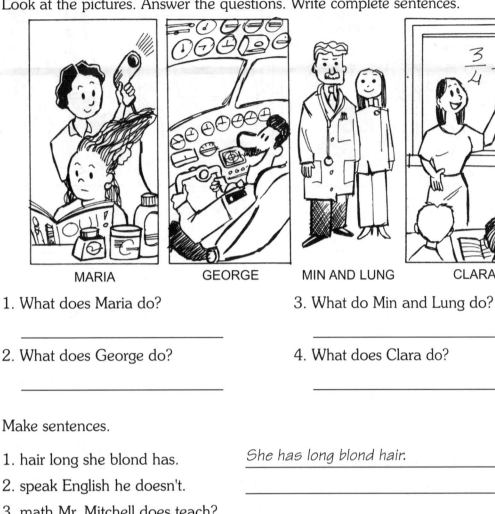

MARIA   GEORGE   MIN AND LUNG   CLARA

1. What does Maria do?

_____

2. What does George do?

_____

3. What do Min and Lung do?

_____

4. What does Clara do?

_____

B Make sentences.

1. hair long she blond has.   *She has long blond hair.* _____

2. speak English he doesn't.   _____

3. math Mr. Mitchell does teach?   _____

4. tall Mrs. Wang is.   _____

5. hair have black does he short?   _____

6. glasses wear you do?   _____

C Put this conversation in the right order. Write numbers.

_____1_____   Let's play tennis on Saturday.

_____   OK. See you Saturday afternoon.

_____   That's fine. I never work in the afternoon.

_____   I usually play at 10:00 in the morning.

_____   What time?

_____   How about Saturday afternoon at 3:00?

_____   That's not OK for me. I always work on Saturday mornings.

D Write about Bill. What are two things he can do? What are two things he can't do?

1. _____   3. _____
2. _____   4. _____

E Now tell about you. What are two things you can do? What are two things you can't do?

1. _____   3. _____
2. _____   4. _____

F Read and answer the questions.

   Karen usually gets up at 7:00 A.M. and gets to work at 8:00. Before work, she always drinks two cups of coffee. At 11:00, Karen reads her e-mail and at 12:00, she eats lunch. She usually eats in the cafeteria, but today she is eating at her desk. She never goes to a restaurant for lunch on Monday through Friday, but on Saturday she always eats lunch or dinner in a restaurant. On Saturday, Karen likes to go to the gym. Then she reads the newspaper and watches TV. Sometimes she goes to the movies. On Sundays, she goes to church, eats a big dinner with her family, and goes to sleep early.

1. What does Karen never do on weekdays?

   _____

2. What are three things she usually does on a weekday?

   _____

3. When does Karen eat in a restaurant?

   _____

4. What does Karen do before work?

   _____

5. What does Karen do after her visit to the gym?

   _____

WHAT DO YOU DO?

Think about what you know. Check (✓) the column.

	I can do this. (+)	I need to study this more. (?)
Say the names of jobs.		
Talk about the jobs of people in your family.		
Ask and answer: *What does (your father) do?*		
Use the simple present tense *(I work, you work, he works, etc.).*		

What do you know now? _____

_____

_____

WHAT DOES HE LOOK LIKE?

Think about what you know. Check (✓) the column.

	I can do this. (+)	I need to study this more. (?)
Say the names of school subjects.		
Say words to describe people *(tall, brown hair, green eyes, etc.).*		
Talk about your teachers and friends. Tell what they look like.		
Ask and answer: *Do you take (math)?*		
Ask and answer: *Do you like (science)?*		
Make negative statements in the simple present tense *(I don't speak French).*		
Use *yes/no* questions and short answers in the simple present tense *(Do you like math? Yes, I do.).*		
Use adjectives in the correct position and order *(short black hair).*		

What do you know now? _____

_____

_____

11 WHAT TIME DO YOU GET UP?

Think about what you know. Check (✓) the column.

	I can do this. (+)	I need to study this more. (?)
Tell the time.		
Talk about your daily schedule.		
Ask and answer: *What time do you usually (get up)?*		
Use the adverbs of frequency: *always, usually, sometimes, never.*		
Know when to use the simple present or the present progressive.		
Use the time expressions: *before, after, then, every day, at, in, on.*		

What do you know now? _____

_____

_____

12 CAN YOU SWIM?

Think about what you know. Check (✓) the column.

	I can do this. (+)	I need to study this more. (?)
Say verbs for outdoor activities *(swim, jog, etc.).*		
Say verbs for leisure activities *(play the piano, play chess).*		
Talk about sports and fun activities.		
Ask and answer: *What do you like to do?*		
Ask and answer: *Can you (play tennis)?*		
Use the modal *can.*		
Use the verb *like* + infinitive.		

What do you know now? _____

_____

_____

I'M GOING TO WEAR MY JEANS

A What words complete the sentences? Write the words in the puzzle.

ACROSS
4. Basketball players wear _____ .
6. Tennis players often wear white shirts with white _____ .
7. In cold weather, you need _____ .
8. _____ are usually blue.

DOWN
1. Women sometimes wear _____ to a party.
2. A man usually wears a _____ with a suit.
3. I always wear _____ with shoes.
4. A T-shirt is one kind of _____ .
5. Boys don't wear _____ .
6. I like to run, and I always wear running _____ .

B One word is different. Cross out that word.

1. shirt	~~jeans~~	blouse	T-shirt
2. shorts	jeans	pants	dress
3. skirt	blouse	tie	dress
4. coat	bathing suit	jacket	sweater
5. shirt	boots	running shoes	sneakers

C Write an affirmative and a negative sentence for each picture.

AMANDA

1. Amanda is going to wear a blouse.

   She isn't going to wear a T-shirt.

ADAM

2. _____

   _____

WINSTON

3. _____

   _____

MANNY AND RUFUS

4. _____

   _____

MEGAN

5. _____

   _____

LARRY

6. _____

   _____

January

Sun	Mon	Tues	Wed	Thur	Fri	Sat
						1
2	3	4	5	6	7	8
9	10	11	12	13	14	15
16	17	18	19	20	21	22
23 30	24 31	25	26	27	28	29

Today
My soccer game
Lisa's party

February

Sun	Mon	Tues	Wed	Thur	Fri	Sat
	1	2	3	4	5	
6	7	8	9	10	11	12
13	14	15	16	17	18	19
20	21	22	23	24	25	26
27	28	29				

concert
English test

D This is Ali's calendar. Tell when he is doing each thing.
Use *tomorrow*, *next week*, and *next month*.

1. Ali   *is going to go to Lisa's party tomorrow.* _____

2. He's _____

3. He's _____

4. He's _____

E What do you think Ali is going to wear to each event? Write your ideas.

1. to Lisa's party   *He's going to wear jeans and a white shirt.* _____

2. to his soccer game   _____

3. to the concert   _____

F Write the words in the correct spaces.

go	going	am	'm	is	's	are	're	be

1. A: ____ you going to go to Lisa's party?

   B: Yes, I ____ .

2. A: What ____ Mary going to wear?

   B: She's _____ to wear jeans and
   a T-shirt.

3. A: Are you going to ____ at 8:00?

   B: No, I ____ not.

4. A: Is the party going to ____ on October 29?

   B: Yes, it ____ .

G Write about yourself.

1. What are your favorite clothes?

_____

2. Do you have a favorite color? What is it?

_____

3. What are you going to wear to school tomorrow?

_____

4. Are you going to wear shoes or sneakers to school?

_____

5. What do you like to wear on weekends?

_____

6. What do you wear in cold weather?

_____

H **WRITING**

A friend is coming to visit you.
Send an e-mail to your friend.

1. Describe the weather.
   Is it going to be hot or cold?

2. Tell the things
   you are going to do.

3. Describe good clothing
   for the visit.

SEND NOW   SEND LATER   SAVE AS DRAFT   ADD ATTACHMENTS   SIGNATURE   CONTACTS

to: _____

subject: _____

message:
_____
_____
_____
_____
_____
_____
_____
_____
_____
_____
_____
_____
_____
_____

LET'S CELEBRATE

A   Maria and Rachel are giving a party. Complete the conversation. Use **want to** or **need to**.

Maria: Let's have a party at my house Friday night.

Rachel: OK. Do you _____ invite all our friends?

Maria: No. The living room is small.
We really _____ have a small party.

Rachel: Are you going to make cookies?

Maria: I _____ make them,
but I _____ ask my mother first.

Rachel: I _____ buy a new sweater for the party.
Do you _____ go to the mall this afternoon?

Maria: I can't. I _____ do my homework.

Rachel: I _____ do my homework too,
but I don't _____ right now.

Maria: Well, let's go to the mall now and do our homework later.

B   Complete the sentences.

1. In the United States, Labor Day is always the *first*____ Monday _____ September.

2. Halloween is party time. It is on _____ _____.

3. Thanksgiving is the fourth Thursday _____ November.

4. Christmas is on _____ _____.

C Maria and Rachel are talking on the phone. They are planning the party. Fill in the blanks. Use *me, you, him, her, it, us,* and *them.*

Rachel: Who are we going to invite?

Maria: Dan is a good DJ.

Let's invite _____ .

Rachel: OK. And Lisa's a good dancer.

Let's invite _____ .

Maria: Carol and her boyfriend,

Aaron, are a lot of fun.

Let's invite _____ .

Rachel: What do we need to buy?

Maria: We need to buy potato chips and fruit.

Let's buy _____ at the supermarket.

My mother is going to drive

_____ to the store.

Rachel: Good. Let's get soda, too.

Everyone likes _____ .

Maria: OK. Do you want to come early?

Rachel: Good idea.

Then I can watch _____ make the cookies!

D Unscramble these sentences.

1. Rachel   and   Maria   us   parties   their   always   invite   to

   _____

2. friends   invite   to   want   they   their

   _____

3. they   go   for   need   to   shopping   food

   _____

4. to   music   want   to   they   have   DJ   a   play

   _____

5. buy   to   want   they   potato chips

   _____

E Look at the pictures. Circle the word in the puzzle for each food.

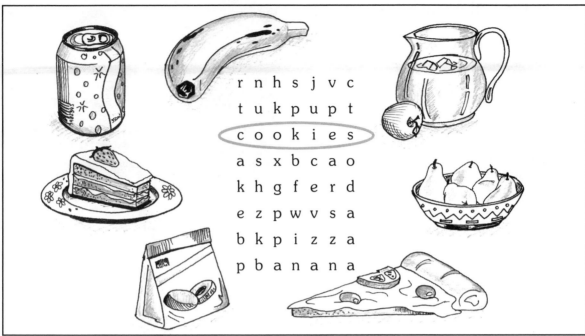

```
r n h s j v c
t u k p u p t
c o o k i e s
a s x b c a o
k h g f e r d
e z p w v s a
b k p i z z a
p b a n a n a
```

F Write the missing word.

1. fifth	_____	seventh
2. eleventh	_____	thirteenth
3. _____	twentieth	twenty-first
4. first	_____	third
5. eighth	ninth	_____
6. fourteenth	_____	sixteenth

G Write the dates. Use words.

Example: August twelfth

When is . . .

- New Year's Day in the United States? _____
- your birthday? _____
- your mother's birthday? _____
- your father's birthday? _____
- your best friend's birthday? _____

H READING

National Holidays

Countries around the world have national holidays. Of course, the holidays are on different days. The ways people celebrate national holidays are sometimes the same.

In the United States, the national holiday is on July fourth. There are many parades with bands and floats. People cook food outside and eat outdoors. In France, the national holiday is on July fourteenth. There are big parades with soldiers, and airplanes fly overhead in the sky. People dance in the streets. Many events are free on that day: you don't need to pay money to go to concerts or operas.

Mexican Independence Day is on September 16th. Everyone from school children to soldiers marches in parades. In Mexico City, there is a huge parade in the main square in the historic district. And everywhere there are bands, *mariachi* music, and dancing in the streets. Many people eat a special Mexican dish, chiles en nogada (peppers stuffed with spicy meat, with a walnut sauce), on this day.

Answer *yes* or *no*.

1. _____ Mexico's Independence Day is on July 14.

2. _____ In the United States, people have parades on July 4.

3. _____ In France, concerts are free on their national holiday.

4. _____ In France, people play mariachi music on Independence Day.

5. _____ In the United States, France, and Mexico, there are parades for Independence Day.

I WRITING

Write about the national holiday in your country.

1. When is the national holiday?

2. Where do people go to celebrate it?

3. What special foods do people eat?

4. What do people do on this day?

5. What is the best thing about this holiday?

The National Holiday in My Country

_____

_____

_____

_____

_____

_____

_____

SHE WAS SMART

Susan and Jim went to this high school.
Ms. Pawski, the principal, tells the students what they were like in high school.

A   Complete the sentences. Use **was, wasn't, were,** and **weren't.**

1. Jim ___wasn't___ good in science. He usually got Cs.

2. He and Susan _____ in the same science class. They had the same teacher.

3. She _____ very good in science. She always got As.

4. They did their homework together. She _____ a big help to him with science.

5. They weren't athletic, and so they _____ on the school sports teams.

6. They _____ always interested in computers.

   Now Susan and Jim have their own Internet company!

B   Change the sentences from negative to affirmative.

1. Jim wasn't good in math in high school.

   _____

2. He wasn't usually late to class.

   _____

3. Susan and Jim weren't in the same science class.

   _____

4. They weren't interested in computers.

   _____

5. Susan and Jim didn't go to the same high school.

   _____

C Complete the sentences. Use **is, are, was,** and **were.** Use words for jobs and activities.

1. John _____ a good student.

   Now he _____ a teacher.

3. They _____ players.

   Now they _____ .

2. April _____ a dancer.

   Now she _____ a dance instructor.

4. Gail _____ player.

   Now she _____.

D Look at the pictures above. Fill in the blanks. Use **has/have, are, had, goes/go,** or **went.**

1. As a child, John _____
   long blond hair.
   Now he _____ short hair.

2. The Smith brothers _____
   to the same school.
   Now they _____ in a rock band.

3. As a girl, Gail _____
   to soccer practice.
   Now she _____ to basketball
   practice.

4. Today April _____ long hair.
   In her teens, she _____ short hair.

66

E READING

Elton John

Elton John is a British singer and writer of songs.

His name wasn't always Elton John. It was Reginald Kenneth Dwight. As a child, Reginald was a very good piano player. His specialty was classical music. Then as a teenager, he had a rock band. By his twenties, he was famous around the world for his rock music. And his name was now Elton John. He was famous, too, for his unusual clothes. His glasses were always in strange colors, sizes, and designs. The shy Reginald was a person of the past.

In the 1970s, Elton had seven number-one albums in four years! In the 1990s, one of Elton John's big successes was the music for the Disney film *The Lion King.* The song "Candle in the Wind" was another very big success. He sang it at the funeral of Princess Diana in 1997.

Elton John is now in his fifties, and his name is still famous around the world for his music.

Answer *yes* or *no.*

1. _____ As a child, Elton John was a good musician.

2. _____ He had strange-looking glasses.

3. _____ He had seventeen number-one albums in four years in the 1970s.

4. _____ He sang at Princess Diana's funeral.

5. _____ He is famous around the world.

Answer the questions. Use short answers.

1. Was Elton John's real name Roger? _____

2. Was he interested in classical music? _____

3. Was he in a rock band? _____

4. Were his clothes strange? _____

5. Was "Candle in the Wind" famous? _____

F WRITING

Describe yourself when you were a child and now. You may use photographs to help you.

> Your picture here.

This is me at age _____.

_____

_____

_____

_____

_____

> Your picture here.

This is me now.

_____

_____

_____

_____

_____

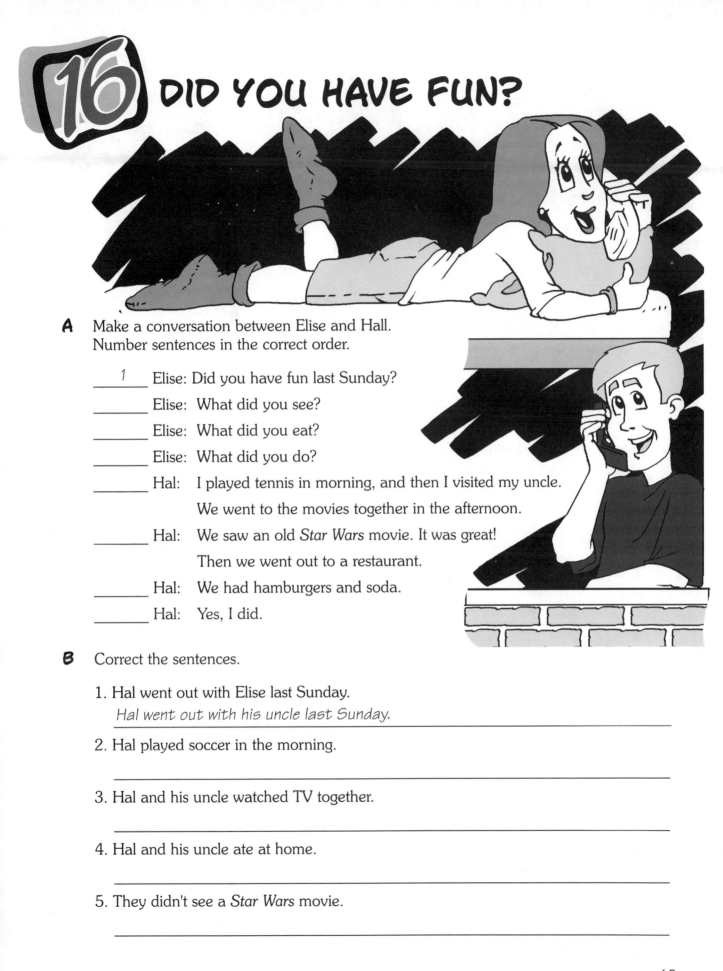

16 DID YOU HAVE FUN?

A Make a conversation between Elise and Hall.
Number sentences in the correct order.

___1___ Elise: Did you have fun last Sunday?

_____ Elise: What did you see?

_____ Elise: What did you eat?

_____ Elise: What did you do?

_____ Hal: I played tennis in morning, and then I visited my uncle.

We went to the movies together in the afternoon.

_____ Hal: We saw an old *Star Wars* movie. It was great!

Then we went out to a restaurant.

_____ Hal: We had hamburgers and soda.

_____ Hal: Yes, I did.

B Correct the sentences.

1. Hal went out with Elise last Sunday.

   Hal went out with his uncle last Sunday.
   _____

2. Hal played soccer in the morning.

   _____

3. Hal and his uncle watched TV together.

   _____

4. Hal and his uncle ate at home.

   _____

5. They didn't *see* a *Star Wars* movie.

   _____

1. last week   3. Monday   5. last night

2. Sunday   4. yesterday   6. this morning

C Estelle was on vacation. Look at the pictures. Tell what she did.
Use the past tense of the verbs in the box.

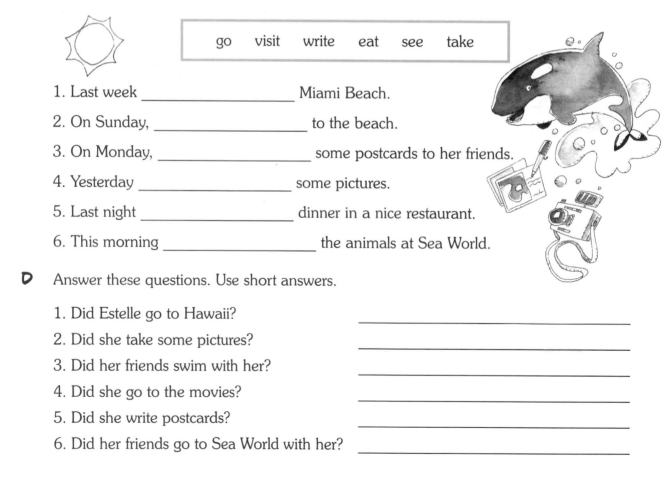

| go   visit   write   eat   see   take |

1. Last week _____ Miami Beach.

2. On Sunday, _____ to the beach.

3. On Monday, _____ some postcards to her friends.

4. Yesterday _____ some pictures.

5. Last night _____ dinner in a nice restaurant.

6. This morning _____ the animals at Sea World.

D Answer these questions. Use short answers.

1. Did Estelle go to Hawaii?   _____

2. Did she take some pictures?   _____

3. Did her friends swim with her?   _____

4. Did she go to the movies?   _____

5. Did she write postcards?   _____

6. Did her friends go to Sea World with her?   _____

Wonder Woman

William Marston created Wonder Woman. In 1941, Wonder Woman was first in a newspaper cartoon. Then, in 1942, Wonder Woman comic books came along. Wonder Woman was the first woman to be a comic book hero. The Wonder Woman comic books were soon very popular.

Wonder Woman came from Paradise Island in the Pacific Ocean. She had special powers. She jumped high and ran very, very fast. She flew in an invisible plane. She also had a magic belt: when she put the belt around someone, the person told the truth. When people needed help, Wonder Woman was there.

Later, there was a television show and several movies with Wonder Woman. Her character changed several times. In the 1960s, she lost some of her powers, but they came back in the 1970s. Today Wonder Woman is still popular. Many people like to watch the old TV shows and read comics with this character.

Answer *yes* or *no*.

1. _____ A woman writer created Wonder Woman.

2. _____ Wonder Woman came from Paradise Island.

3. _____ The first Wonder Woman stories were in newspapers.

4. _____ Wonder Woman had a magic belt.

5. _____ Wonder Woman lost some of her powers in the 1960s.

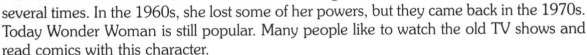

F Change the sentences from negative to affirmative.

1. A man didn't write the Wonder Woman comics.

_____

2. Wonder Woman didn't help people.

_____

3. There wasn't a Wonder Woman TV show.

_____

4. She didn't fly in an invisible plane.

_____

5. Her character didn't change.

_____

G Write the past tense of the verbs. Then circle the words in the puzzle.

PRESENT TENSE	PAST TENSE
go	_____
have	_____
do	_____
clean	_____
write	_____
see	_____
paint	_____
drink	_____

```
s  t  h  a  d  w  r  o  t  e
s  a  w  c  l  e  a  n  e  d
f  y  d  i  l  c  s  w  q  l
s  r  i  t  i  p  l  e  s  c
a  g  d  s  e  y  w  n  w  y
d  r  a  n  k  w  v  t  z  r
p  a  i  n  t  e  d  w  t  w
```

H WRITING

Send an e-mail to a friend.
Write about a special day in your life.

1. How did the day start?

2. Who was with you?

3. Where did you go?

4. What did you do?

5. What was the best part of the day?

6. How was the day special?

SEND NOW   SEND LATER   SAVE AS DRAFT   ADD ATTACHMENTS   SIGNATURE   CONTACTS

to: _____

subject: _____

message:

_____

_____

_____

_____

_____

_____